Newsfeed Ads

B. Vincent

Published by RWG Publishing, 2021.

NEWSFEED ADS

First edition. August 10, 2021.

Written by B. Vincent.

Also by B. Vincent

Affiliate Marketing
Affiliate Marketing
Affiliate Marketing

Standalone
Business Employee Discipline
Affiliate Recruiting
Business Layoffs & Firings
Business and Entrepreneur Guide
Business Remote Workforce
Career Transition
Project Management
Precision Targeting
Professional Development
Strategic Planning
Content Marketing
Imminent List Building
Getting Past GateKeepers
Banner Ads

Bookkeeping
Bridge Pages
Business Acquisition
Business Bogging
Marketing Automation
Better Meetings
Conversion Optimization
Creative Solutions
Employee Recruitment
Startup Capital
Employee Mentoring
Followership
Servant Leadership
Human Resources
Team Building
Freelancing
Funnel Building
Geo Targeting
Goal Setting
Immanent List Building
Lead Generation
Leadership Course
Leadership Transition
LinkedIn Ads
LinkedIn Marketing
Messenger Marketing
New Management
Newsfeed Ads

Table of Contents

Newsfeed Ads

Welcome to this seminar on newsfeed promoting. In this course, we will cover how to drive designated traffic from Facebook with local promotions. This course is partitioned into three modules, module one covers showcasing goals, module two covers crowd advertisement arrangement and spending plans and module three covers making the genuine promotion itself. When this course is finished. You'll realize how to adequately make and dispatch Facebook promotion lobbies for your business. So right away, we should jump into the main module. Alright, folks, welcome to module one. In this module, our master will show you the different promoting goals and how to pick the best ones for your business. So, prepare to take a few notes and how about we directly hop in.

Module One

Welcome to module one where we'll be Going over. Promotion targets. First thing you'll need to do is come up to business chief, all devices, and promotions director. Next, we'll tap on the make button. This will carry us to the advertising objective. Presently, a many individuals like to simply make a plunge here in light of the fact that they're amped up for getting their advertisement crusade running and they go with traffic since traffic seems like it has wide application. Notwithstanding, that is an enormous misstep. You truly need to plunk down, ponder your advertising targets and objectives, and pick the right showcasing objective. Prior to pushing ahead with your advertisement crusade, we should go through a portion of the more normal ones. Brand mindfulness is fundamentally about getting your item or your administration or your image personality. All the more explicitly before whatever number individuals as would be prudent inside your specialty or your ideal crowd reach then again is comparable, however it's not going for a specific sort of individuals or kind of segment.

So, reach would be essentially for items with expansive allure. In case you're beginning, for instance, a vacuum cleaner organization or a filtered water organization that applies to everybody. Thus, reach may be a keen choice all things considered. Nonetheless, in case you're selling mechanical copiers or fax machines or something to that effect, clearly your ideal crowd is somewhat more special. Thus, you'll need to go with brand mindfulness. The following target class is thought. The first of these is traffic. This is presumably the most well-known one that individuals consider driving traffic from Facebook over to your web properties, regardless of whether it be a lead page, a business page, your site, or some substance. Presently there's a couple of various kinds of thought other than traffic that many individuals don't ponder again and again. Commitment is intended to get precisely that commitment likes follows shares on your genuine Facebook content application. Introduces.

In case you're in the versatile application, industry is likewise a choice under the thought classification, video sees for video content, in case your is video content hefty or video content driven, or on the other hand in the event that you have viral substance that you're trusting will expand the scope of your image, then, at that point video sees is a decent evenhanded to pick lead age. This really permits you to make lead catch Facebook promotions, Facebook lead advertisements inside the newsfeed that don't expect individuals to leave Facebook. Also, this is an extremely incredible, generally new apparatus messages are another amazing methodology and likely the freshest huge pattern in Facebook advertising. As of late with these, you can really kick discussions off with possibilities and expected clients within Facebook courier and really influence Facebook courier as a promoting and deals stage. Next there's transformation. This classification is likely what you need to investigate.

In case you're truly searching for primary concern income, age deals, in case you're doing transformation rate enhancement, in case you're driving traffic through channels and you're attempting to make a self-exchanging offer that sort of thing, changes are not the same as broad traffic since you're driving explicit kinds of activities within your web properties or across various pages of web properties. Furthermore, Facebook will really change and influence your promotion execution dependent on these objectives and with the assistance of transformation following, which is additionally given by Facebook next there's index deals. Presently these promotions will naturally show things from your internet business store. So, on the off chance that you have a Shopify store or a WooCommerce store or something to that effect, you can really have your intended interest group. See your advertisements for explicit items from your store with negligible manual work on your part. This is an extraordinary chance in case you're running an internet business store and you need to drive leads and likely deals from Facebook lastly their store visits, which fundamentally implies people walking through, not advanced, yet pedestrian activity, attempting to get Facebook clients who are some place neighborhoods to you to come into your genuine business environment. So, there's a great deal of incredible advertising targets here. Facebook has worked effectively in the course of the most recent couple of long stretches of tweaking the way that it spreads out its promoting goals and adjusting its advertisements to your targets, to assist you with getting the best presentation and the best outcomes for each dollar you spend on your Facebook Advertising efforts.

So, to keep things as wide as could really be expected, we will go with traffic for this model, we'll make our mission named traffic zero one. We'll hit proceed, and we'll continue on to focusing in the following module.

Module Two

Hello people, welcome to module two. In this module, our master will cover crowd focusing on advertisement position and planning. So, prepare to take a few notes and we should directly bounce in.

Good, welcome to module two, or we will be going over traffic position and spending plan. So before getting to this point, clearly you should have done some market or crowd research. You need to have a symbol of the best client or a possibility that you need to pursue with your Facebook advertisements. So, for this model, suppose we are making another games drink and we need to get our new games drink before individuals in the wellness specialty. For areas, you can get extremely inventive here. Assuming we needed to, we could simply leave it comprehensively at the United States. How about we feel free to go with one explicit, OK, when you pick a city, you can really go with a span around that city. Presently for our motivations, how about we simply say, we're attempting to sell our games drink to anybody in the United States. So, we'll pick the United States in general.

Presently I haven't looked into the wellness specialty yet suppose that we did. Also, that our exploration demonstrated that ages 21 to 44 were the most dynamic purchasers of sports drinks inside our crowd. Next sex. We could pick one of these.

We'll set it to all dialects, not actually a factor here, but rather assuming you need it to, you could pick explicit dialects. And afterward for nitty gritty focusing on, we can really jump considerably more profound and ensure we're hitting the ideal individuals. We should simply type in the word wellness and see what occurs. So, Facebook is now giving us a ton of proposed interests, practices, and even businesses and occupation titles that we can pick here. Wellness experts may be keen on our games drinks so we could pick that actual wellness as an overall interest has a tremendous after 311 million. That may really be excessively wide. So, we should go with men's wellness somewhat more restricted and right, how about we see what we get with ladies' wellness. For this situation, as should be obvious, we have practices and interests to browse. We can really go with ladies' design and attire purchasers. Ladies' attire, ladies' wellness plans, yet the genuine brilliant piece in this rundown of recommended focusing on will be Women's wellbeing and wellness magazine.

Ladies who have been recognized by Facebook as having revenue in this magazine are an exceptionally amazing business sector to pursue for wellness item. It's not simply somebody who previously enjoyed a page that had something to do with wellness. This is a particular brand, a genuine magazine that exists. And afterward we can envision that individual who are recorded by Facebook as being keen on it would even be supporters of the magazine or if nothing else devoted devotees via web-based media. So, suppose that we're acceptable with this arrangement of focusing on here. Suppose we need to limit it considerably further. Suppose 3,500,000 is excessively huge of a compass for us on our first promotion run. For reasons unknown, how about we go excessively limited, and we'll type in another interest. How about we attempt rec center and wellness clubs. Presently, when we picked that our crowd contracted to 150,000 individuals, and that is on the grounds that Facebook uses and rationale rather than oral rationale between these two boxes here, we're narrowing.

So, for this situation, anyone who needs to be in our crowd should be a piece of this crowd and any of these three, as opposed to this one or this one or this one or this one, that is the thing that narrowing does three amazing. For this situation, we really limited our crowd a smidgen to an extreme so we can click X to eliminate that and rationale, and we'll continue forward with our 3.5 million individuals, potential reach continuing on to positions. It's turning out to be increasingly more prescribed to pick programmed positions on the grounds that Facebook as a stage is exceptionally brilliant. It realizes what will get you the best outcomes more often than not, assuming you need it to come in here and physically pick your positions. Suppose you have a genuine functional justification just needing individuals on versatile or just needing your advertisement to appear in the newsfeed rather than the sidebar or just needing your promotion on Instagram.

You could positively come through here and mark, each of these, you may have a justification this having to do with your crowd research. Maybe you discovered that the most dynamic buyers of sports drinks make their buys on cell phones. Presently that doesn't sound likely, however similarly for instance, you may have a valid justification for doing this. Be that as it may, first of all, you should allow Facebook to do the truly difficult work here and go with programmed arrangements. Also, after you've run your initial a couple of missions, then, at that point you can think back and see which situations performed best, and afterward start physically picking those later on. For this situation, you're facing the challenge out and allowing Facebook to do all the difficult work on your several missions. Furthermore, you can utilize that information later on to cause your promotions to perform significantly more proficiently. So, we should continue on to spending plan.

Presently, spending plan is an inconceivably significant factor of your mission to get, right, since it will fundamentally influence the exhibition of your mission. Presently, the principal choice to make is day by day versus lifetime. If you somehow managed to go with a lifetime spending plan, you'd essentially be setting a maximum add up to be spent during a particular timeframe for your promotion crusade. In case you're going with an evergreen methodology, which means your offer, won't lapse, or you're not working with a hard dispatch period, day by day financial plan may be ideal. What's more, essentially, you'll be choosing the amount you need to spend each week. For this situation. Presently how about we move to run my promotion set constantly beginning today. You'll see, for this situation, you'll spend close to 140 every week, except the day-by-day sum will shift. Facebook will just ensure that the normal across every week is roughly $20, however you may spend somewhat more than that, or somewhat less than that each day.

In the event that you pick a beginning and end date, nonetheless, Facebook will naturally compute the aggregate sum that you will have spent before the finish of that advertisement crusade. So once more, it comes down to whether you're working with a hard dispatch or a terminating offer or a real evergreen offer that doesn't lapse following up. We should discuss improvement for the promotion conveyance. This is extremely cool. What's more, very Facebook has as of late figured out the way that a great deal of snaps that individuals pay for don't really transform into genuine site sees. So how about we read through this truly fast, to make sure we comprehend Facebook permits you to upgrade now for greeting page sees, to discover more individuals in your intended interest group who will tap on your advertisement and pay attention to this and hang tight for the presentation page to stack Facebook is really following the assistance of change pixels, etc. the exhibition and the conduct of individuals after they click from Facebook and head out to the a great many points of arrival out there.

Also, they know with their calculations and with their information, what sort of individuals are bound to tap on a presentation page that is pertinent to them and sit tight for it to stack. Also, what sort of individuals are bound to click once and in a flash skip since they're not able to trust that the page will stack, which is a shockingly enormous measure of individuals. So, suppose we're going for snaps to presentation pages rather than simply broad expansive snaps. Presently, different choices here would have been impressions, which fundamentally you're simply paying for the number of individuals will really see your promotion in their newsfeed or spring up in their sidebar. Etc. or every day special reach, which essentially sets a greatest for individuals to see your promotions a one time each day. Presently we'll nail with finish online visits with the end goal of this model bid sum.

So, this ought to be passed on to programmed, particularly in case you're new to Facebook advertisements, you're allowing Facebook to do the truly difficult work by and by, similarly as we are with positions, and they will sort out what the most ideal bid technique is. Try not to stress over picking this and believing that Facebook will scam you and make you pay more than you ought to be for your Facebook, realizes that the better presentation and better bang you get for your buck, the almost certain you will be to keep giving them more cash. So, they will ensure that your advertisements function comparable to conceivable. Presently, assuming you needed to go the manual course, you really need to pick your bid sum and set it per presentation page see. Once more, that is a real view, not simply a tick. In case you've been doing this for some time, and you know, your numbers truly well, suppose you have a business pipe set up, a lead age, and a business channel, and you've effectively determined the lifetime worth of each client and the possible worth of each lead.

Also, you have a thought of the amount you're willing to spend per presentation page see to gain a lead and realize without a doubt that you'll make back the initial investment or come out with a benefit dependent on a specific bid sum. Well then, at that point go on by all means and go with manual. Nonetheless, on the off chance that you don't have the entirety of that information previously set up, in the event that you haven't done all the numerical as of now, and in case you're new to Facebook advertisements, strongly suggest you go with programmed and let Facebook do the entirety of that numerical and algorithmic hard work for you. Presently with the greeting page sees improvement alternative, we will get charged for impressions. Furthermore, presently the set as the default, be that as it may, if you somehow happened to pick an alternate choice, you'd see an additional alternatives interface here, and you'd have the option to pick things like certain activities, for example, clicking a connection, or on the other hand in case this was a Facebook lead promotion we're setting up, it would be for each time somebody really answers their email address and turns into a lead.

Presently we don't have advertisement planning picked here on the grounds that we have our day-by-day spending set. In the event that we had set this to lifetime spending plan, we'd have the option to control our real promotion planning conveyance type. It fixes a standard now, which means show your advertisements for the duration of the day on your chose plan. In any case, assuming we needed to, we could go with the sped-up alternative on the off chance that we had manual offers going on. What's more, that implies the accentuation has put on the speed at which your promotions are displayed to whatever number individuals as could reasonably be expected. So that covers this module. We went over traffic focusing on and situations and financial plan and timetable. Presently we will continue on to making our genuine advertisement inventive.

Module Three

H ello people, welcome to module three. In this module, our master will cover crowd focusing on advertisement situation and planning. So, prepare to take a few notes and we should directly bounce in. Good. Welcome to module three. In this module, our master will help you about how to make the genuine advertisement itself. So, prepare to take a few notes and how about we directly hop in.

Okay folks. So here we are on the advertisements innovative page. OK. Presently the inventive alludes to in a real sense the advertisement picture or media in addition to the content. Alright. The genuine thing that will be seen by your possibilities and the alternatives for the advertisement inventive have detonated over the most recent couple of years, as should be obvious, there's a ton of various things that you can do truth be told, more, most as of late you can transform pictures into recordings. There's continually something new here. Furthermore, when you see this video, there's most likely going to be some lovely cool new stuff also. Presently we should go through every one of the various organizations actually rapidly. So merry go round, you can have numerous pictures or recordings now, OK. That look from left to right, individuals can go through and here's a little review of various positions and perspectives.

What's more, as you can see that all by itself has gotten pretty extended. There's a huge load of spots. Individuals can see your promotions, alright. Yet, in case you were taking a gander at it on your work area newsfeed, that is what a merry go round would resemble. You're simply going through photographs or recordings, right.

What's more, on portable, Lou would resemble that. So, the following alternative here, single picture, this is the most established, the Oldie, however goodie still, as I would see it, quite possibly the most impressive ones, a great many people ought to simply be utilizing this for effortlessness. What's more, that is the thing that we'll do also, except if you're running an internet business store or something. In which case you know, assortment may be significant. We'll get to that in a second or video, obviously is likewise very, incredibly amazing too. Picture or video. One of these two is the thing that by far most of you will wind up utilizing. So single picture, extremely fundamental. The picture isn't the promotion and that is vital. A many individuals come in here and they believe they will take a picture. Furthermore, they will have a lot of text in the picture, you know, attempting to pass on their message. That is not how it functions. Indeed, your range can really go down extensively on the off chance that you have an excessive amount of text in your picture, alright. They disposed of the old standard where your advertisement would be objected in the event that it included over 20% content, which was somewhat difficult to delineate. You used to need to utilize a little ruler and ensure you would see little quadrants or segments. Furthermore, it would advise you if your writings took up over 20% of You of your promotion, however presently as opposed to objecting, they just, they simply influence your compass, which isn't, bad. You know, you wanna ensure you amplify your range. So, the picture isn't the promotion. It's vital. You need a convincing picture that makes individuals pause and look, and afterward the promotion is in the duplicate. Alright. It's in the content. Okay. I see a many individuals attempting to do Facebook promotions and the content is barely anything. A few Lines. And afterward the promotion is in that general area, and They attempt to crush, you know, the same amount of text as could really be expected yet stay inside 20%. What's more, and that is simply not how Facebook advertisements work. That is bad practice for Facebook advertisements. OK. So, we'll presumably wind up utilizing this for our model today, yet first how about we go on to a solitary video.

Alright. Fundamental video promotion. OK. It says prescribed length as long as 15 seconds. You can go Longer. Alright. In any case, if you need the maximum reach and retainability, you know, holding individuals' eyeballs on your video then the 15 seconds as long as 15 seconds is acceptable. They're, they're suggesting short messages, short, however sweet messages that get individuals to make a move. Right. And furthermore, having the more limited length expands the odds that it will actually want to appear on situations, different arrangements also. So, for Facebook 240 max is really long, yet for Instagram, you'll see here. That is really short, 120 seconds. OK. So, you're restricted there to simply two minutes in length, or it will not have the option to appear on Instagram, in the event that you decide, in the event that you picked that as a situation remunerated video is the last one where you have real limitations on position and that is 30 to 60 seconds. So, in case you're keen on these positions, you need to attempt to make it as short as could really be expected.

Assuming not, hey, pull out all the stops. 240 minutes. Why not? Right. the following choice here is a slideshow. Alright. It's fundamentally a video promotion that circles through a lot of pictures. Alright. You can show a three to 10 pictures and a video as long as 15 seconds in length and it's quite cool. OK. I see a ton of those assortment is generally, I mean, a many individuals might actually utilize this, yet typically assortment is internet business alright. Where you have an assortment of numerous actual items with a series or a line of items, and you need to grandstand those then the, you could utilize gather. So, we will go with a solitary picture for our advertisement, and we will look on down and we must pick a picture. Presently you can pick free stock pictures from here inside Facebook, which is really sweet. So, we're Going to say we are offering telephone bringing or telephone deals to a close administration. OK. So how about we feel free to type a telephone and see what that brings us.

There we go, Dude, on a telephone, that is basically all we need. Alright. It's a gorgeous stock picture and that is actually all we need. So how about we come on here to message on the glue in some duplicate. Presently this duplicate you'll see is long. That should be locked. Indeed, it very well may be any longer than this. OK. This is somewhat short as, as espresso goes among the you know, those aware of everything about how Facebook promotions Should function.

Presently this takes individuals through fundamentally a substance piece, nearly. It's similar to a small-scale blog entry and fix a few mistakes here. Furthermore, it fundamentally takes individuals through a tedious clarification of why they ought to be keen on the thing we're advertising. Alright. This entire castigation here is about deals as opposed to shutting. Alright. Furthermore, how selling and the customary idea of deals needs to stop. Every one of the old deal's stunts need to stop. Also, a smarter Approach called shutting is the thing that you should use on the telephone Then in your business. Alright. Furthermore, fundamentally at the end, there is a source of inspiration. Snap, learn more to snatch our free aide on high ticket shutting. Furthermore, obviously that brings them as a lead into our framework. You know, this is, we're actually fantasizing here. So, all things considered we can offer them subsequently, our end telephone shutting administrations, isn't that so? How about we come on here.

H T P S Shutting Done right.com, which is certainly not A genuine URL, or perhaps it is a URL as far as I might be aware, But I recently made that up on the spot. A feature Headline will be quit Selling, begin shutting, which sounds somewhat odd, your normal individual who isn't intrigued or doesn't know about the qualification there will pause and say, stand by, what are they discussing? Quit selling, begin shutting.

Source of inspiration. Learn more works for us since we really referenced that in our duplicate, however you have a lot of various alternatives here. Apply. Presently, peer down for calls. You can go with no catch by any means. In the event that you'd like a get in touch with us give presently, download, get, offer, get cites, loads of various ones that may be appropriate to your promotion. Also, that is pretty much it, we could really push ahead with this with no guarantees. There are some different alternatives. Assuming you need it to really show the site, the web address on the advertisement down here, you could really put that here. Alright. So, we could snatch an end done, correct? Show that here then individuals would then have the option to see that in the promotion. And afterward we could put a portrayal, which is similar to a little, little form of the duplicate. Simply kind of a review of what we're discussing here, right there. Alright. Furthermore, it's simply one more lump Of, of writings to get individuals more inspired by your application. That is pretty much it we've Got our promotion duplicate. We have our promotion picture. We've Got every one of the subtleties down here, set up. We have connecting to our site, and we should view what this resembles in every one of the various situations. So, this is portable Newsfeed, not terrible.

Obviously, the watermarks will be taken out once the advertisement is distributed. Furthermore, this is work area newsfeed, Instant articles, isn't that so? Segment portable commercial center, Facebook stories, your Instagram channel, Instagram stories, crowd, organization, crowd organization, medium square shape crowd organization, local more crowd organization,

Obviously. Gracious. What's more, we have the expert inbox, which is a later turn of events. However, talking about ongoing improvements Facebook's crowd network is for sure at developing. What's more, that is the reason we have such countless new arrangements dependent on where, on what gadgets and where around the web your advertisements can be seen through their organization. So that is practically it. This is the stopping point for us. We just hit affirm, and our advertisement will be live.

Don't miss out!

Visit the website below and you can sign up to receive emails whenever B. Vincent publishes a new book. There's no charge and no obligation.

https://books2read.com/r/B-A-QWUO-DBDRB

BOOKS 2 READ

Connecting independent readers to independent writers.

Also by B. Vincent

Affiliate Marketing
Affiliate Marketing
Affiliate Marketing

Standalone
Business Employee Discipline
Affiliate Recruiting
Business Layoffs & Firings
Business and Entrepreneur Guide
Business Remote Workforce
Career Transition
Project Management
Precision Targeting
Professional Development
Strategic Planning
Content Marketing
Imminent List Building
Getting Past GateKeepers
Banner Ads

Bookkeeping
Bridge Pages
Business Acquisition
Business Bogging
Marketing Automation
Better Meetings
Conversion Optimization
Creative Solutions
Employee Recruitment
Startup Capital
Employee Mentoring
Followership
Servant Leadership
Human Resources
Team Building
Freelancing
Funnel Building
Geo Targeting
Goal Setting
Immanent List Building
Lead Generation
Leadership Course
Leadership Transition
LinkedIn Ads
LinkedIn Marketing
Messenger Marketing
New Management
Newsfeed Ads

About the Publisher

Accepting manuscripts in the most categories. We love to help people get their words available to the world.

Revival Waves of Glory focus is to provide more options to be published. We do traditional paperbacks, hardcovers, audio books and ebooks all over the world. A traditional royalty-based publisher that offers self-publishing options, Revival Waves provides a very author friendly and transparent publishing process, with President Bill Vincent involved in the full process of your book. Send us your manuscript and we will contact you as soon as possible.

Contact: Bill Vincent at rwgpublishing@yahoo.com www.rwgpublishing.com

www.ingramcontent.com/pod-product-compliance
Lightning Source LLC
Chambersburg PA
CBHW022115210326
41597CB00048B/1172